A SERIES OF ESSAYS
ABOUT MENTAL HEALTH

By Luke Eveling

For Paul and Jane - Good blokes x

And Mum - Thank you for literally everything over the past 9 months. Love you x

Mrs Mackenzie was pretty good to me too

PROLOGUE - THE SUMMER OF 2019 AND THE GREAT GATSBY

"He was silent, and I guessed at his unutterable depression.
'I feel so far away from her,' he said. 'It's hard to make her understand.' - this is from F scott Fitzgerald's novel the Great Gatsby
The first time I read this quote... well it didn't really resonate with me at all. To me at the first time of reading this, it could've one of those throwaway quotes in a book you read all the time. Like 'Snowball took no interest in Napoleon's meetings' or 'Harry hated his uncle for that' a quote

in a famous book that could just as easily have been removed as quickly as it was written down. No need for it.

I was 14 when I read the quote for the first time, and at the time, life was amazing.
I had developed an identity and relationships with people that were healthy and at the time, sustainable. My fears and insecurities about my weight had evaporated and for only one of a few times in my life, I didn't have a single worry or sadness; the relationship, trust and general love my Mum and I had was not only mutually balanced but we got on a lot too. I also had just started the first relationship of

my life with a girl. I would ̄
doing the summer justice b
trying to describe it, but yo̧
the Gist, I really really likeᴄ
summer.
I had this almost juvenile
disregard for any wrongdᴄ
but at the same time was given
almost all adult freedoms with
my life.
It felt like in the summer of 2019,
that life and happiness went
hand in hand and were a
constant like gravity, I felt like
this girl and I battled against the
societal norms of times for
14/15/16 year olds (alcohol,
drugs etc)
Most moments of my time with
her at the time were like not
much I had felt before and I don't

think I'll feel for a pretty long
time again.
 2019 was the best year of my life
so far.

 But reading this for the second
time 18 months later and coming
up to my 16th birthday I noticed
the quote properly.
So much has changed since the
summer of 2019, to begin with
the girl and I are not together
anymore and she has moved on
to someone new. I battle with
very severe depression along
with other disorders such as an
eating disorder and Asperger's
syndrome.
I'm not going to lie, life is harder,
and worse in many ways. I'm
very lonely due to losing friends

and not many things give me pleasure. But life is bearable, I mean, I wouldn't be writing this essay at school if it wasn't and hopefully it will continue to slowly go in this direction.

But as I read this quote for the second time, the sentimentality of it changed. This surreal feeling of two periods paralleling (2019 and now). It made me feel lonely, because with the exclusion of more honesty in my life, my general standard of happiness was different. The summer of 2019 is becoming so far away and it meant less and less to other people but more and more to me as I try hold onto the feeling.

And to me this was depressing. I am very desperate most moments to return to this Summer and a time where things are so much different and life was good, a feeling that my friends truly want to be with me and the feeling of seeing a girl you like and getting butterflies and knowing the feeling is mutual. This absolute feeling that you are appreciated and loved. Because I know, from first hand experience, to feel rejected and to miss the love of life so dearly, well... it can drive one insane.

This is where a few nights ago at 2am I struck a similarity between myself and Jay Gatsby. He loved Daisy so much but could not achieve the thing he so desperately needed. Ultimately, I feel all Jay Gatsby wanted was to be appreciated and understood just as we all would like to be. He missed the past so much and it was his only passion to return to it, and I feel the same way.

To finish this essay I would like to say that through my recent issues and experiences, I have learnt one thing. That life goes on, time can be for myself and Jay Gatsby's case is something that creates space on a period you wished you could grab and hold forever, but also time is a healer.
Time creates new spaces for happiness; I'm only 16, I still

have much time left and you always need to look forward to the other feelings you'll have in life, not behind.

THE BURDEN AND BEAUTY
OF NOT FEELING

If I had to describe what unsurity
of I am feeling is like, I'd say it's
like walking through the world
during a storm, without an
umbrella, unsure if you'll be able
to find shelter.
When you see friends, you
double guess everything,
Thinking 'was that right to say?'
or 'when should I speak?' Life
becomes very frustrating when
you can't identify how you feel
properly, you think it'd be
probably better if you stayed
home as the general hum of
frustration hits your gut.

This can be exhausting, mentally, and physically. You wait all day until you can find a safe space where all interactions cease to exist. A space where you can finally take your eyes off the cloud of thoughts in your head, and lie there uninterrupted, watching something.

Before I was formally introduced to aspergers, I called it by a bunch of other names, such as - overthinking, tired, and just a bad temper. My ex called it 'being able to flip a leaf quickly' and my Mum called it being 'all brains no common sense.' but we were all wrong.
It overwhelmed me because it meant that there wasn't a

tornado of character flaws falling on me and that there was an actual medical thing going on in my head. My diagnosis in many ways kickstarted me getting better; I stopped taking drugs, I tried to get some form of work into my life at the time, and started trying to instead of thinking 'what is wrong with me?' began to accept my complex and annoying state of mind for what it is. I buckled down and did every step of therapy Paul and Jane (my two therapists) wanted to do with me.

And after a while of doing this, I started to feel. Nothing makes you feel more deliberately alive than feeling something. Like

Crying with someone because you don't want to see your brother hurt, or feeling genuine empathy for your mothers struggles at work, or the nirvana of eating your favourite meal. Or even the hot wave of flirtation that comes over you when a fit girl holds her gaze on you for a bit too long.

For someone with aspergers to have a morsel of understanding for how they feel can be a gift, but unlike many others. My ability to feel things isn't always constant.

I try to see aspergers as a gift, and in many ways it is, I mean, I feel I would not be able to write

in this way if it wasn't for my
condition, but the faceless
frustration of not being able to
feel things can be this tornadic,
frustrational pain too.
If I have learnt one thing with my
journey with aspergers is that
feeling is a gift, and a life without
these things can be achievable.
I appreciate the slumps of
feelings when I come out of them
because it reminds me how lucky
I am to be alive and in many
ways the best part of having
aspergers is that relieving feeling.
You always need to face things
with the feeling 'this is tricky, but
I've got this.'

I MISS BEING A DICKHEAD

26, Forth Street Edinburgh, first floor, is funnily enough in many ways the floor that is most important to me in my life now. My councillors floor.

Therapy is a real luxury. The freedom to speak about whatever you want for 50 minutes can be a special and priceless thing. And it also means after a time, no life cancelling depression.

So I feel pretty nervous when I consider leaving my councillor when I have clarity, and I mean true clarity of mind. Sometimes I wished I could go back to being a dickhead.

I miss being a dickhead sometimes, I had a sense of identity, that now I have to try and rebuild in myself that I had built for many years. Of course it goes without saying that I don't miss the way I treated people, but it does feel like big chunks of me are missing in my identity, and when you lose those big chunks of yourself, life becomes a little meaningless. I miss thinking that there were double meanings under everything and modelling my life in a way that was like the godfather. When you begin to live a kind of diet coke life. You can occasionally feel the same narcissistic joy that you once had like when you're listening to a rap song for example, but overall, the balanced and reasonable mind is empty much of the time and boring. There are upsides though, I can now text my friend Lewis without thinking I'm texting my *consigliere*. I can now realise things for how they are and take things at face value. But it's just not as fun.

I do totally agree with what I've just written, but I still feel like I'm missing out - like without therapy I could return to this fun and excitement. I now face the question of who I am. I'm quite good at writing, I think, I'm pretty smart, a little bit autistic (the perfect amount) pretty lazy and have a slow metabolism is

what I am, and that is all I'll ever
be at the core, which is boring
but secure, I'm now united like
the rest of society with a boring
identity. And although I like
being secure, I also like the
simple fantasy of being a
dickhead.

FEELING SAD IN MY KITCHEN

The last time I felt sad was... well it was today. At 1:31pm in my kitchen, but 8 hours later I feel able to bear my depression for one of the first times properly in my life.

I was diagnosed with depression 8 months ago now. And I can remember it like it was yesterday; clenching a tissue in my hand as the doctor told me the bad news. Since then life has been hard for me, constantly trying to navigate my feelings is very draining for anyone, when the smallest frustration can lead me to overthink and feel depressed it can make me feel like my emotions are enormous.

Things have been on the up though, it would be a lie to say that my life, mood and ability to deal with things hasn't steadily improved. When I'm emotional I do not look around to find something to blame and violently put it out on other people anymore, Now I usually try and rationalize what's going on and process them in a quiet and civilized way. But I'm prone to outbursts sometimes, whether it'd be over being asked to undo the dishwasher by my Mum, or seeing my Ex Girlfriend in a relatioship with another person. Even when I'm able to process

things in a good way, the final
outcome is still the same -
sadness.

Pre therapy was all I ever knew
about sadness and emotions -
and it was bad.

This is where I found myself in
the evening puzzled at being able
to rationalize and feel happy after
being sad. The sadness that
usually follows was instead
replaced with a clarity of mind
that I haven't encountered a lot
in my depression. My view of
happiness seemed to have
changed.

As a society, we aren't allowed to
be sad, happiness is an integral

part of western culture, you cannot live a fulfilling life if you are not happy. This is reflected in my personality pre therapy. I always pushed away this emotion that was justified for me to feel. You are told to 'wipe away the tears and get on with it' and continuously block out a feeling that is natural to express.

So tonight, instead of being able to be happy at my ability to be able to feel things in a productive way, I found myself saying 'what is wrong with me?'

AN ESSAY ABOUT HEARTBREAK

Everyone experiences heartbreak. It's an inevitable part of human existence and life is heartbreaking. It's meant to be, and is rooted in our emotional makeup.

I love... A lot. Hard. Fiercely. Unconditionally. If you're loved by me you know it. Loving has always come natural to me, I love to love. I'm here to love everyone. To almost be love. Because of how much I love people, I find it hard losing people. I lost once, the love of my life at the time, my confidant, my greatest friend, the type of person that probably comes around twice in your life, someone who becomes your identity and your makeup.

When I lost that person it felt like I had lost part of myself, like 50% of me had diminished through a text message, I felt empty and Hollow.

My heartbreak brought about immense grief that I still have to deal with today, literally losing someone forever made me feel alone and like I'd rather not be alive. The complexity of my heart was too overwhelming for me to feel at the time and this heartbreak had arrived to hurt my soul.

Looking back on the early days of that heartbreak, I found the whole feeling uncomfortable. I didn't want to feel this emotion so I ran away from it, into the pool of other girls.

I felt like the vulnerability was a sign of weakness on my part. I was trying to run away from a feeling that was natural to express and in many ways almost a month on from that I still do that, but I'm proud of how I'm handling the pain now generally, because it goes against all the things I was taught growing up in societyuy72   `. I try to now process the emotions and allow myself to understand things better, but it's still hard, because I'm going against everything that seems easy. I try to put it out in my writing now, and try to transfer the passion and love I felt for this girl into other things, like schoolwork and family time.

Because there is more. Love can leave us so confused and desperate for answers, but what this recent heartbreak has taught me that there is an opportunity, an opportunity for me to grow emotionally from this experience and make me a stronger and better person than I was before. Because this pain doesn't define us.
Our love does.

THE FOUR STAGES OF GETTING OVER SOMEONE

Emotions are such a worrying concept. Like when you think about it, biologically they are our worst enemy. They stray us for the most part and leave us in our society, from doing the overall right and logical thing.

I know I've mentioned heartbreak a lot so far, but that's because in many ways it symbolises how non malleable our emotions really are. With heartbreak, (and other emotions) we are overcome with this wave of loss and our judgment is all of

a sudden so hazy and startlingly
shit when looking back.

The media portrays men in this
very bachelor heavy light. And
while that may remain valid for
some men, it's not always the
case - especially if the
relationship was great. After all it
is human nature to want to love
and be loved.

So I compiled a stage by stage
process of heartbreak and tried
to sum up all human heartbreak
for the modern man in a 4 stage
process.
/
/
/

Phase 1: Her loss. Myself and many men have huge egos. And at the time, we let ourselves believe that this was more of a loss for her. In many ways I still carry some of the characteristics of this phase today. Of course you can't keep living like this, and eventually the ceiling will fall, We may seem fine but on the contrary however the unutterable constant of rejection is there. We just choose to ignore the feeling.

Phase 2: Social Butterfly. Unlike most women, men don't internalise the rejection at first. I guess we try to sweep it under the rug naturally and move on. You talk to loads of girls. A huge amount. It can be a very disheartening period for the male as the pain can be confusing, and this seems the best way out but in many ways - it isn't.

Phase 3: realisation. Now that the social roar of phase 2 is over, a certain amount of realization comes over you as everything is questioned. From the reason of rejection up to what led to it, everything comes into serious existential questioning and that can lead to a lot of anger and sadness, but at the same time because you're beginning to confront what has been swept under the rug for so long. It's actually you confronting the rejection.

Phase 4: Acceptance. This is an acceptance that it is finally over and you have nothing to gain from the other person. You may even want to still get back with her at this point, but you realise that life can be so much more fruitful without her. You begin to heal and understand yourself without this other person being such a huge influence on your emotional makeup.

And there you have it - A complete compilation from my heartbroken self on the stages of heartbreak. Of course this is a massive generalization of people's emotional stages and whatnot as we are all different, but I feel it does follow a general theme on how we work as human beings over such an unnatural emotion.

If I can make you draw one thing off of this jovial generalization of heartbreak is that; many times life moves on. Life continues and as a whole without this person, life can be a beautiful thing when you aren't reliant on someone else. You feel 100% as an individual, instead of being split as 50/50.

BACON ROLL

I had a bacon roll for break at
school today. And I can't stop
thinking about it. Ok wait, let me
explain.

Up until now, I've only eaten
what other people closest to me
ate.

Ever since I was old enough to
formulate a decision on what I
should eat, I always felt
influenced by what other people
consumed for break at school like
it was some sort of unwritten rule
to eat what the others did as
though it was my obligation to
adhere to the unwritten rules of
food I had set in my head.

8 months ago, I was diagnosed with depression. Subsequently, I was diagnosed with Asperger's syndrome.
After many thousands of pounds later I am not burdened with these things such as peer pressure and as a result, many of the things that had been such a problem have slowly become a lesser issue over time.

So sincerely; I do not take the buying of this bacon roll lightly, because after a lot of retraining, I was able for the first time to free myself from peer pressure.

Peer pressure can be legitimately problematic, absolutely problematic in fact. If your social anxiety comes from an illogical or a non obvious place about doing something that feels natural but at the same time unnatural for you to do if you're with certain people it can make you feel very suppressed from personal experience. Of course you can't keep living like that, but culturally we are taught to be enticed by conformity even when dissent is natural.

I can't describe in an essay how I finally managed to get to the position of picking up the bacon roll instead of just a water, it would take me a lot of writing to sum up how I did it, but I CAN sum up that it took me 8 months, of 2 different therapists, 4 months off school, Thousands of pounds and lots of pain, to heal to the point of a bacon roll at break.

WRITER'S BLOCK

I've started a ritual to allow myself to write garbage or non integral personal essays when in writer's block. It involves me saying whenever I'm overthinking my writing ability 'you're allowed to write shit essays Luke.'

I say it when I'm not completely confident of my writing ability but want to write, like when reading F. Scott Fitzgerald's *The Great Gatsby* with his beautiful descriptive language, or being mesmerized by Drake lyrical ability while listening to his song *4PM in Calabasas*.

It's mostly a joke. A loving dig at
how easy it can be for me to write
shit and non integral essays. But
also it's an emotional cleansing;
by thinking this it almost
reminds me that I'm human and
it allows me to seize a fleeting
idea and pin it down.

But soon, I begin to feel the
emotional pressure to make my
mental health my rhetorical ever
present underlying theme to all
my essays. This is very much self
inflicted, due to the type of book
I'm writing but now, when I'm
writing about my mental health
for the most part I found myself
unable to make an essay that I'm

proud of, or come to a clear, concise and beautiful conclusion.

Things become very tricky when you're tied up in this identity claim, you can offer your pain up in a handful of essays and if you try and make yourself write about it again, it seems morally disingenuous.

The pressure I put on myself to write about my mental health due to my book, puts myself at great risk of being emotionally pigeonholed as a writer, and as a whole I'd be wrongfully contributing to the newly emerging subgenre that is youth mental health literature (if that even could be called a literary subgenre).

When I feel pressured to write not only now does it give my essays a smell of writer's block, but also it just makes them no longer valid to the sensitive subject of mental health either.

I want to let myself one day be able to not be held to the shackles of mental health as a writer, because mental health as a subject is already draining and I don't want that to be reflected in my writing either, because it de-validates the concept of mental health not only on paper but in life.

I'll try to continue to keep an eye on the emotional integrity of my work and try not to create clickbait writing. Alongside 'You're allowed to write shit essays Luke' I can try and remind myself of what writing is all about - explaining myself to myself whether I'm writing about a bacon roll at break, heartbreak, depression, autism. Or the issue of writer's block.

A SHORT BIT ABOUT THE PAST

I can't stop thinking about the past and all the people in it.

Not so much the fact of the past, but really the connotations of it - the manner of the past, the places, and sights and smells of the past. Some days I'm so drawn into the past to the point of complete mental paralysis. I spend my day drawing everything back to the past and it can be exhausting. Having to live a normal life with this on top of you.

I have been working to try and limit this morbidity with my

counsellor for the best part of a year now, and while they are limited in their amount a lot more, they are still very much there. I wish for a day where I can go wherever I want, and speak to whoever I want without feeling drawn back to specific parts of my life.

I can now recognise these thoughts a lot more now and the patterns of them before they become too big of a burden on my day, but it doesn't make the anxiety itself less likely. I still get the anxiety in shorter, less potent spurts and through therapy, I've been able to rationalize away my anxieties but it still doesn't feel like that is still enough of a sufficient reason to stop fearing the past.

It's probably safe to say my autism makes me afraid of the past, but I know in many ways I'm not unique in my fear. Maybe I experience it in a more disruptive way than others and they have a better ability due to their neurotypicality to put it to the back of their minds.

But there's something very safe in feeling like I'm not alone, like these feelings won't only subside for me, but for the vast majority of the teenage population, and I've found the best relief comes from setting those thoughts free -

thinking 'one time this was the
past, but today is now.'

EPILOGUE - THE GREAT GATSBY AND SUICIDE

"Gatsby believed in the green light, the orgastic future that year by year recedes before us. It eluded us then but that's no matter - Tomorrow we will run faster, stretch out our arms farther . . . And one fine morning - So we beat on, boats against the current, ceaselessly into the past."

The first time I read this quote I was once again, 14, very content and happy. Enjoying all the summer of 2019 had to offer for me. I had a girlfriend that I loved very much and life was good.

The quote at the time struck me as a paragraph of literature that was deeply profound, but I didn't have the emotional depth or understanding to realise it's true meaning or it's beauty.

And only now, after all the things I've been through am I able to realise the pain in this quote.

Writing this book, in many ways, saved my life. When I began writing the first essay (the prologue) I felt in many ways my existence had been exhausted. I felt like giving it all up and killing myself. But writing this book began to heal the pain I had for so long felt about life. It gave me this physical material outlet that even therapy couldn't give me. It made me feel like for the first time in my life that there was an existential meaning to it and that I meant something and for someone that is depressed, it means more than anything to have that.

So when I was thinking of what to write for the epilogue of my book, I found myself once again reading the great gatsby.

And while reading this quote and the book I realised how far I had actually come as an individual since the beginning of writing my book 55 days ago. I realized that I have healed.

Because the green light is in all of us. It is a hope of something far greater than what is in our reach, is in our reach, it is the idea that we need to forever continue as individuals because ultimately that is all we can do - continue.

We are all rocks on the shore ceaselessly taking batterings from the sea and wind and I find comfort in that - the idea that if I were to kill myself, everything would continue after a period of time and that as a fact, almost gives me an incentive to stick around as an individual, and fight the demons in my life, because that is what that quote and more importantly, this book I have written has taught me;

that there is always a light at the end of the tunnel and that life is beautifully continuous.

THE END